KICK, JUMP, CHEER!

CHEERLEADING SQUADS

BY SARA GREEN

BELLWETHER MEDIA • MINNEAPOLIS, MN

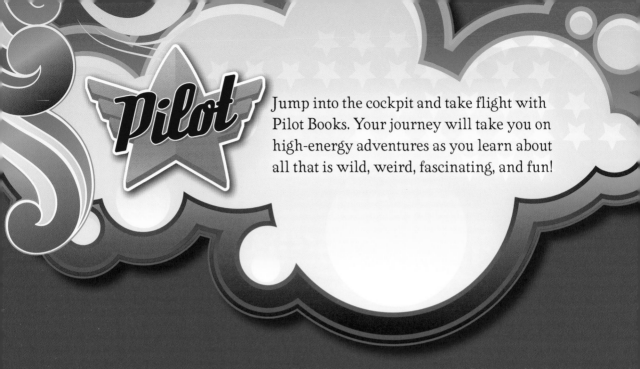

Jump into the cockpit and take flight with Pilot Books. Your journey will take you on high-energy adventures as you learn about all that is wild, weird, fascinating, and fun!

This edition first published in 2012 by Bellwether Media, Inc.

No part of this publication may be reproduced in whole or in part without written permission of the publisher.
For information regarding permission, write to Bellwether Media, Inc., Attention: Permissions Department,
5357 Penn Avenue South, Minneapolis, MN 55419.

Library of Congress Cataloging-in-Publication Data
Green, Sara, 1964–
 Cheerleading squads / by Sara Green.
    p. cm. — (Pilot books: kick, jump, cheer!)
 Includes bibliographical references and index.
 Summary: "Engaging images accompany information about cheerleading squads. The combination of high-interest subject matter and narrative text is intended for students in grades 3 through 7"— Provided by publisher.
 ISBN 978-1-60014-650-3 (hardcover : alk. paper)
 1. Cheerleading—Juvenile literature. I. Title.
 LB3635.G745 2011
 791.6'4—dc22   2011010384

Printed in the United States of America, North Mankato, MN.

080111   1187

CONTENTS

TEAMING UP

It's the first cheerleading practice of the year. You can't wait to meet your **squad**. You've always wanted to be part of a team. Your squad will spend a lot of time together at practices, games, and other events. One of your squad's first tasks will be to set goals. Everyone will work together to achieve them. Goals might include raising school spirit to a new high, entering a cheerleading competition, or learning a difficult **stunt**. Setting goals means your squad will face challenges. Team members must learn to trust each other and **cooperate**. Squads that practice good teamwork are more likely to reach their goals, stay safe, and have fun.

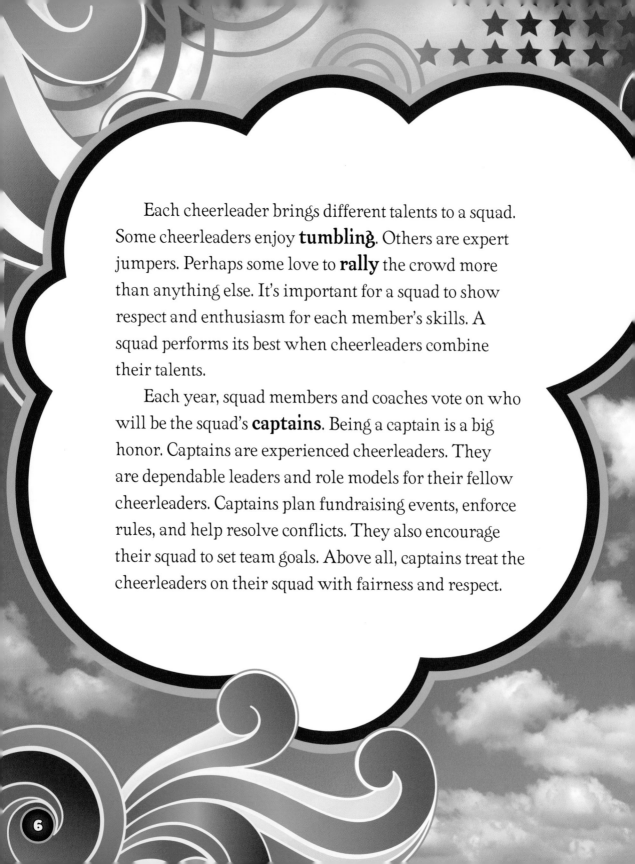

Each cheerleader brings different talents to a squad. Some cheerleaders enjoy **tumbling**. Others are expert jumpers. Perhaps some love to **rally** the crowd more than anything else. It's important for a squad to show respect and enthusiasm for each member's skills. A squad performs its best when cheerleaders combine their talents.

Each year, squad members and coaches vote on who will be the squad's **captains**. Being a captain is a big honor. Captains are experienced cheerleaders. They are dependable leaders and role models for their fellow cheerleaders. Captains plan fundraising events, enforce rules, and help resolve conflicts. They also encourage their squad to set team goals. Above all, captains treat the cheerleaders on their squad with fairness and respect.

Many squads create their own rulebooks. The rules cover topics such as grades, practice attendance, and where cheerleaders can and cannot wear their uniforms.

WORKING TOGETHER

Squads show a high level of teamwork when they perform stunts. Coaches assign cheerleaders to one of three important roles. **Bases** keep their feet on the ground at all times. They are usually the strongest and tallest cheerleaders on a squad. Bases lift and throw cheerleaders called **flyers**. The flyers must be able to move high in the air with ease. They are often the smallest and lightest cheerleaders on the squad. **Spotters** have the most important job in a stunt. They keep everyone safe. If a base looks shaky, spotters step in to help support the flyer. If a flyer falls, spotters are there to catch her. Stunts are thrilling to perform when everyone works together!

BUILDING FRIENDSHIPS

A great way to strengthen the bonds between members of a squad is to do team-building activities during practices. These fun games help cheerleaders learn to trust one another. They also help build friendships. You might discover new things about your teammates and find that you have a lot in common!

TEAM-BUILDING ACTIVITIES

MINEFIELD Objects, or "mines," are scattered on the ground. The cheerleaders pair up, and one partner is blindfolded. The cheerleader who can see uses only her voice to guide her partner through the minefield.

LINE UP Divide the squad into two teams. The teams race each other to line up in order of birth date. The challenge is to do this without talking.

WOULD YOU RATHER? In this game, cheerleaders take turns asking the squad questions beginning with "Would you rather…." Would you rather go to Antarctica or the Sahara Desert? Would you rather eat only pizza or only tacos for the rest of your life? Cheerleaders go to different sides of the room, depending on their answers. They share the reasons for their answers before starting the next round.

It's important for your squad to spend time together outside of practices and performances. Getting to know each other on a personal level will strengthen your friendships. You will look forward to cheering together even more. Here are a few ideas for your next get-together.

SQUAD ACTIVITIES

DANCE-OFF

Get together to perform your top moves to your favorite songs. Show off your singing talents at the same time!

MOVIE NIGHT

Invite everyone to bring over a favorite movie. Pop some popcorn and settle in for a night of films and fun.

VOLUNTEER

Offer to teach basic cheerleading skills at a local elementary school. Your squad will have a great time teaching fun chants and cheers. The kids will love it too!

FUNDRAISING

Hold a bake sale or a car wash to raise money for your squad. Use the money to buy uniforms, accessories, or other equipment.

RAISING SCHOOL SPIRIT

Members of a squad must work together to raise school spirit at **pep rallies**. These gatherings usually take place at school before important sporting events. Cheerleaders get the students and athletes excited for the games. Pep rallies are even more fun when squads get teachers and school staff involved!

PEP RALLY IDEAS

TEAM CHEER
Teach a few chants, cheers, and easy stunts to the members of a sports team. Have them perform for the crowd!

THEME
Come up with a theme for the pep rally. How about a beach theme? Toss beach balls into the bleachers and teach the crowd a hula dance.

DANCE CONTEST
Have a teacher-student dance contest. A group of teachers and a group of students dance to a song at the same time. Cheerleaders ask the crowd to applaud each group separately. The group that gets the loudest applause wins!

Cheerleading squads raise school spirit in other creative ways. Squads often surprise athletes by decorating their lockers before big games. Decorations can include colorful ribbons, wrapping paper, and even candy. Adding banners that display encouraging phrases such as "You Can Do It!" is a nice touch.

Squads enjoy getting students involved in raising spirit. Many squads organize contests for the best original school flag. The winning flag is displayed in school. Some squads help each grade create their own **chant** or song. Students yell them at pep rallies, games, or other school events. Squads might also organize a spirit week leading up to an important game. For example, they might encourage students to dress in clothes from a different decade each day of the week.

SUMMER FUN

Your squad can get a head start on cheering by attending a summer cheerleading camp. Squads go to camp to strengthen team bonds, learn new skills, and practice **routines**. Squads can choose to attend different kinds of camps. **Resident camps** last three to five days. They are often held on university **campuses**. Cheerleaders stay overnight at resident camps. **Day camps** usually last one to five days. Cheerleaders spend each day at camp but return home at night. **Private camps** are held at a squad's school. Instructors come to the school to work one-on-one with a squad.

Participating in camp traditions is a fun part of camp. One common tradition is for squads to yell chants as they move from one activity to another. At resident camps, squads decorate their rooms in creative ways. Some squads cover their doors in wrapping paper.

THREE CHEERS FOR TEAM PLAYERS

Great cheerleaders are team players. They always put the squad's needs first. Team players listen to their coaches, follow directions, and treat other cheerleaders with respect. They also have a positive attitude and look for the best in others. When conflicts come up, team players look for solutions that benefit the entire squad.

For team players, being on a cheerleading squad is exciting. It's all about raising school spirit, encouraging sports teams, and involving the crowds at games. It's also about teamwork and building friendships. Squads look better than ever when they work as a team!

GLOSSARY

bases—cheerleaders who lift and support flyers; bases keep their feet on the ground at all times during a stunt.

campuses—the buildings and grounds of colleges and universities

captains—the leaders of a sports team; cheerleading captains help coaches lead practices and plan events.

chant—a short, repetitive phrase yelled during a game

cooperate—to work together to achieve a goal

day camps—cheerleading camps held during the day; day camps usually last one to five days.

flyers—cheerleaders who stand on the bases and jump or are tossed into the air

pep rallies—gatherings held before sporting events to boost school spirit and encourage sports teams

private camps—cheerleading camps held in the privacy of a squad's school; cheerleaders receive one-on-one instruction from camp staff.

rally—to stir up and encourage enthusiasm

resident camps—overnight cheerleading camps that usually last three to five days

routines—sequences of moves that cheerleaders practice and perform

spotters—cheerleaders who are ready to help the bases catch flyers

squad—a group of cheerleaders that works together as a team

stunt—a cheerleading move that involves climbing and lifting; in some stunts cheerleaders are thrown into the air.

tumbling—gymnastics skills such as cartwheels and handsprings; many cheerleading squads use tumbling in their routines.

TO LEARN MORE

At the Library

Crossingham, John. *Cheerleading in Action.* New York, N.Y.: Crabtree Pub. Co., 2003.

Gruber, Beth. *Cheerleading for Fun.* Minneapolis, Minn.: Compass Point Books, 2004.

Jones, Jen. *Cheer Squad: Building Spirit and Getting Along.* Mankato, Minn.: Capstone Press, 2006.

On the Web

Learning more about cheerleading is as easy as 1, 2, 3.

1. Go to www.factsurfer.com.

2. Enter "cheerleading" into the search box.

3. Click the "Surf" button and you will see a list of related Web sites.

With factsurfer.com, finding more information is just a click away.

INDEX

The images in this book are reproduced throug
the courtesy of: James Hajjar, front cover, pp.
9, 19, 21; Andrew Rich/Getty Images, p. 5; Tor.
Carter/Alamy, p. 11; Mike Kemp/Photolibrary,
p. 12; Eric Gay/AP Images, pp. 14-15; Getty
Images, p. 17.